Zara Spook and Other Lures

by

Joan Ackermann

SAMUEL FRENCH, INC.
45 West 25th Street NEW YORK 10010
7623 Sunset Boulevard HOLLYWOOD 90046
LONDON TORONTO

ISBN 0 573 69216 5 Printed in U.S.A. #28002

TO MY PARENTS,

BAR AND KURT

IMPORTANT BILLING AND CREDIT REQUIREMENTS

All producers of ZARA SPOOK AND OTHER LURES *must* give credit to the Author of the Play in all programs distributed in connection with performances of the Play and in all instances in which the title of the Play appears for purposes of advertising, publicizing or otherwise exploiting the Play and/or a production. The name of the Author *must* also appear on a separate line, on which no other name appears, immediately following the title, and *must* appear in size of type not less than fifty percent the size of the title type.

In addition to the above the following credit must also be shown:

> "Professional premiere at Actors Theatre of Louisville. Originally produced at Mixed Company, Great Barrington, Mass."

Zara Spook and Other Lures was originally presented by Mixed Company in August 1989, directed by Robert Russell. The cast (in order of appearance):

TALMADGE........................... Daniel Osman
EVELYN .... Irene McDonnell
TEALE............................. Joan Ackermann
MARGERY .... Gillian Seidl
MEL.............................Thom Whaley-Wool
RAMONA .... Lisa Nicole Wolpe

Zara Spook and Other Lures professionally premiered at the Actors Theatre of Louisville, March 1990 directed by Kyle Donnelly. The cast (in order of appearance):

TALMADGE.......................... David Chandler
EVELYN .... Anne O'Sullivan
TEALE............................. Joan Ackermann
MARGERY .... Priscilla Shanks
MEL.......................... V Craig Heidenreich
RAMONA .... Annette Helde

CHARACTERS
(in order of appearance)

TALMADGE, mid-thirties

EVELYN, thirty

TEALE, late thirties

RAMONA, late thirties, forty

MEL, forty

MARGERY, forty-five

TIME: The present.

PLACE: The play takes place in West Virginia, in Truth or Consequences, New Mexico, and on the road in between.

SET

This play seems to work best with a very simple set. The car and truck can be suggested with chairs; perhaps a grill in front with headlights, and a steering wheel mounted on a board on the floor. The boat that Evelyn and Teale fish in doesn't even need an outline. Two boat seats on the floor and their equipment is enough. The farther downstage it is played the better so that Evelyn is practically casting into the audience. She can use one rod with no line for most of the scene, and right before her last cast, she can pick up another rod with a line fixed to the floor so the rod can bend, indicating she has caught a fish. In all scenes, the lake is best played out front where the audience sits. Once designers start defining little pools on the stage, they limit the spectator's vision of a huge lake. There's no need for painted blue water or actual mountains. A large handsome backdrop of a New Mexico sky and imaginative lighting can suggest more than any paper-mâché butte. Good country-western music can help the transitions during the black-outs between each scene. There should definitely be country-western playing while the audience enters and during intermission.

NOTE: Having heard many readings of this play, I have learned that these six characters are not quickly accessible. It's important that Talmadge be manly, not wimpy or whiny. He is driven by his love for Evelyn who is struggling to find herself. His scene with Mel is not about male bonding; they connect across a wide gap, but the gap remains. In the second scene, Mel is not interested in Margery. His focus is on Ramona in the car in front of him, mistakenly assuming she is romantically linked to Talmadge. Ramona has a robust love for life and an expansive generosity of spirit. Because of her asthma,

Teale hasn't fished the tour or left her home in months and is apprehensive about surviving this trip. All the characters face their worst fears, suffer loss of control, regain it, encounter moments of grace and compassion from total strangers, and ultimately expand their horizons in New Mexico, land of infinite horizons.

ZARA SPOOK AND OTHER LURES

ACT I

Scene 1

It is five in the morning in Evelyn and Talmadge's bedroom in Beckley, West Virginia. EVELYN is asleep. TALMADGE tip-toes in, carrying a breakfast tray with food and presents on it. HE is wearing a jacket over his pajamas. HE sits down on the edge of the bed with the tray on his knees and looks at EVELYN who has pushed the covers down off her chest. HE pulls them back up over her. SHE pushes them down again. HE pulls them back up. HE grabs a waffle from the tray, dunks it into a glass of orange juice and sucks on it, studying her. HE picks up phone from the bedside table and dials.

TALMADGE. (*Talking quietly.*) When are you coming over? Huh? It's Talmadge, who did you think it was. Could you wait a sec? I dropped my waffle. My *waffle,* wait. Damn. Teale, when you coming over? Uh-huh, well, Evelyn asked me to call you? She's running a little behind schedule here and wonders if you could make it a little later. Maybe an hour or two. Two hours, three, something like that? Huh? She asked me to call you. Yes, she did. Why am I talking so soft? I always talk soft in the early morning hours, Teale. I get louder as the day goes on. So we'll see you later, much later. Appreciate it. (*Hangs up phone.*)

(*ALARM CLOCK goes off.*)

EVELYN. (*Sitting bolt upright.*) I'm awake!

TALMADGE. Surprise!

(*EVELYN gets up to turn off clock which is positioned strategically away from bed.*)

TALMADGE. Surprise going away party! Come on back to bed, Evie. What'll it be? Waffles or pop-tarts?

(*Another ALARM CLOCK goes off on the other side of the room. EVELYN goes to it.*)

TALMADGE. (*Picking up box.*) Frosted or plain.

EVELYN. Talmadge, I had a bad dream …

TALMADGE. Apple cinnamon. Your favorite. And this cup of coffee has got your name on it. Right here. See?

EVELYN. My name?

TALMADGE. (*Reads.*) "Evie darling."

EVELYN. Fingernail polish. Aw, that's sweet. Don't put it in the dishwasher, Talmadge, the letters will steam away.

TALMADGE. Come on back to bed.

EVELYN. I can't. Teale's coming. Where's my cap? Oh, I had such a vivid bad dream.

TALMADGE. Come on, sweetheart. I'm not gonna see you for a whole week. Here, come and open your presents.

How about this one, you want to open this one? See the balloon? Evie?

EVELYN. It's nice. It's a nice balloon, Talmadge. Decorative.

TALMADGE. You can take it with you. It's got my breath in it. (*Holds up small present.*) Guess what this is.

EVELYN. I remember. I was out fishing in the tournament and I caught this … fish … and when I reeled it in … it had this weird blue electric typewriter in it, an IBM Selectric, the kind with the ball that swivels? In its mouth? I don't know but the fish, Talmadge, the fish was typing me. Not with its fingers. Typing the way I do, in my mind? He was typing me I had done something … wrong … something bad I can't remember and … this fish with the ball turning was announcing it like on a p.a. system? All across the lake by typing, so loud everyone, Ramona, everyone could hear my … failure. Am I making sense?

TALMADGE. (*Nods.*) Uh-huh.

EVELYN. What do you think it means, a dream like that?

TALMADGE. I don't know, but you're headed for rain tomorrow, sweetheart. Make sure you and Teale take turns every two hours.

EVELYN. What a dream to embark on a two thousand mile drive with.

TALMADGE. And if the rain gets too heavy just pull over.

EVELYN. I have been typing again, Talmadge.

TALMADGE. I know. It's okay.

EVELYN. Not really.

(Third ALARM goes off. Perhaps in chest of drawers, or inside closet. EVELYN goes to turn it off.)

TALMADGE. Three?

EVELYN. We have to leave by five-thirty in order to pick Ramona up at the airport seven-twenty pm the nineteenth day after tomorrow.

TALMADGE. That Ramona certainly has the world by the balls, doesn't she. You talk about her like she hung the moon.

EVELYN. Do you know what an honor it is to drive Ramona to the Classic? What an honor? How come you're wearing your coat?

TALMADGE. I went out to check the car a few times. Evie, that back right tire, you got to keep an eye on it. Every time you fill up I want you to ask the man at the filling station to look at it and see if it has enough air, okay?

EVELYN. Okay.

TALMADGE. And if the clutch gets a little squishy again just put some of that brake fluid in, I showed you where. The little cup not the big one. I marked them with a green magic marker, B for brake C for clutch.

EVELYN. What'll I do if I don't catch a fish at all, Talmadge, if I don't catch even one little bitty fish. I'll be mortified.

TALMADGE. You can always ask the man at the filling station to put it in for you.

EVELYN. The fish?

TALMADGE. He'll know how. He's done it before.

EVELYN. Did you put my tackle box back in the car?

TALMADGE. Uh-huh.

EVELYN. Why did you take it out again?

TALMADGE. (*Holding up present.*) What do you think this is?

EVELYN. I don't know.

TALMADGE. Guess. (*SHE takes it and starts slowly unwrapping it.*) It's a cassette.

EVELYN. Oh.

TALMADGE. But what cassette? Who's on the cassette? That's the surprise.

EVELYN. I don't want to tear the paper …

TALMADGE. Forget the paper, I didn't give you the paper, Evie …

EVELYN. I've got to get dressed. Oo, my stomach's all flibbety flubbety. Do you know, I suspect I'm almost more excited about making the drive than I am about the tournament. Isn't that silly?

TALMADGE. Forget the paper, We're never going to use that particular piece of paper again.

EVELYN. I've never driven so far by myself.

TALMADGE. We have other paper for other presents.

EVELYN. It's come to be real important to me. Making this trip?

TALMADGE. Here, give it to me. (*Grabs present, rips off paper.*)

EVELYN. (*Starts getting dressed, putting clothes on under her nightgown.*) I remember the first time I drove from Beckley to Charleston after Addie moved there? I had to pull over every fifteen minutes just to catch my breath. 'Course, I'd just gotten my license. End of May; five months ago.

TALMADGE. (*Holds it up.*) See?

EVELYN. A cassette.

TALMADGE. Uh-huh.

EVELYN. Nice.

TALMADGE. But what cassette? *Who's* on the cassette?

EVELYN. I don't know.

TALMADGE. Here.

EVELYN. (*Takes it while changing, looks at it.*) Crystal Gayle.

TALMADGE. Crystal Gayle. Not Crystal Gayle. Does that look like Crystal Gayle? It's me. I'm on the cassette. I made it for you to listen to while you're driving.

EVELYN. Aw. You are really, really thoughtful, Talmadge.

TALMADGE. You want to listen to some now?

EVELYN. I'll save it for the road.

TALMADGE. That's okay, I'll play you a little bit right now. (*Has a cassette player right on table, puts in cassette—him, singing romantic country western song.*)

EVELYN. I'm going to the Classic, Talmadge. The Bass'n Gal Classic, Elephant Butte Reservoir, Truth or Consequences, New Mexico. Oop, my heart just did a little back flip. That's not you.

TALMADGE. It is too, it's me.

EVELYN. Go on.

TALMADGE. It's me.

EVELYN. Truly?

TALMADGE. Yeah. Yes.

EVELYN. What do you know.

TALMADGE. That's Grady's band backing me up. Like it?

EVELYN. It's different.

TALMADGE. Both sides, sixty minutes. (*Pause, watching her.*) You're so pretty, Evie. Are you going to change like that after we're married. Evie?

EVELYN. Huh?

TALMADGE. I said are you going to change like that after we're married? Dressing under your nightgown.

EVELYN. Oh.

TEALE. (*Calling from offstage.*) Evelyn! I'm here!

EVELYN. (*Looking at her watch.*) Right on time.

TALMADGE. Bless her heart.

EVELYN. Well, I guess we're going.

TALMADGE. Going?

EVELYN. Wish me luck.

TALMADGE. Evie ...

EVELYN. That tuna casserole, just pop it in the microwave. There's Lean Cuisine in the freezer and turkey roll and Spam for sandwiches. I typed out menus for seven days it's on the fridge.

TALMADGE. I might have a fever.

EVELYN. And Gladys and Birdy are having you over for dinner Tuesday night, don't forget.

TALMADGE. Fine.

EVELYN. They'll be real disappointed if you don't come.

TALMADGE. I will. I like Norman and Susie.

EVELYN. Not Norman and Susie. Gladys and Birdy.

TALMADGE. Gladys and Birdy. That's who I was picturing. Gladys and Birdy.

EVELYN. Remember, Gladys just had her tubes tied.

TALMADGE. I'll remember.

EVELYN. She's apt to be a little sore.

TALMADGE. I'll be careful.

EVELYN. Where's my new Rand McNally road Atlas? (*Remembers she put it under her pillow.*) Oh, here it is. (*Takes it out.*)

(TEALE enters. SHE is fearful and apprehensive about the trip.)

TEALE. Hey, everyone.
EVELYN. Hey, Teale.
TALMADGE. Teale.
TEALE. Talmadge.
EVELYN. All set? Ready to make some history?
TALMADGE. History? Without me?
TEALE. What are y'all listening to?
EVELYN. Talmadge. That's Grady's band backing him up.
TEALE. Mm. That's why.
TALMADGE. That's why what?
TEALE. It sounds like that.

(TALMADGE takes cassette out; gives it to Evelyn.)

EVELYN. I'll call you tonight, eight o'clock your time.
TALMADGE. What do you mean my time?
EVELYN. Your time'll be different from mine. I'll be in a different time zone. Teale, are you as jittery as I am? I know you are.
TEALE. I'm gonna give you some of my medicine, Evelyn; for back up.
EVELYN. Okay.
TALMADGE. A different time zone.

EVELYN. I think I still have the last batch you gave me, Teale. (*Takes a bottle of pills out of her pocket book.*) I do.

TALMADGE. You've never been in a different time zone before.

EVELYN. See my new driving gloves?

TEALE. Sharp.

(TALMADGE utters a sound of pain.)

EVELYN. Did you say something?

TALMADGE. Fine. (*Smiles.*)

EVELYN. (*Kisses him.*) Bye, Talmadge.

(TEALE exits.
TALMADGE holds Evelyn.)

EVELYN. I'll miss you. Thanks for my going away parties. All of them. I really appreciate them.

TALMADGE. Bye.

EVELYN. You okay?

TALMADGE. Fine.

EVELYN. Bye.

TALMADGE. Bye.

EVELYN. Can I really do this? Two thousand miles?

(HE nods, gives her a positive gesture. SHE kisses him again and leaves. TALMADGE stays sitting rigidly on bed, trying to contain himself. HE falls over. TEALE enters.)

TEALE. Talmadge, could you take those videos back? They're gonna cancel my membership. You've had "Blue Lagoon" out over a month. Talmadge?

(HE nods. SHE leaves. Sound of CAR ENGINE starting up.)

TALMADGE. (*Sits up.*) Evie. (*Pause.*) Evelyn! Evelyn!! (*HE bolts from the room.*)

Scene 2

It is NIGHT TIME, two days later on Highway 25 between Albuquerque and Truth or Consequences, New Mexico. The scene alternates between the interiors of a car and a pick-up truck. TALMADGE (still in pajamas) is driving, EVELYN beside him; RAMONA sits behind Evelyn and TEALE behind Talmadge. TEALE plays every now and then on her banjo for a little bit. MEL and MARGERY are in the truck.

TALMADGE. Evelyn? Evie, honey, you all right? That's okay. You don't have to talk if you don't want to.

———

MARGERY. I do so appreciate your giving me a ride.

MEL. No trouble.

MARGERY. What are you going to do down in Elephant Butte?

MEL. Business.

MARGERY. Oh?

TALMADGE. Well, hot spit. I got a peanut here has four peanuts in it. What do you know. Unless I made a mistake. Nope ... I don't think so. Four. Uh-huh. All from the same peanut. So ... anybody too cold? (*No response.*) Too warm? Huh-huh. (*Cheerily.*) Fine.

MARGERY. Well, that car is far from home. West Virginia. What part of New Mexico are you from?

MEL. Little town north of Taos.

MARGERY. Taos. How marvelous to grow up in such a magical place. What was it like?

MEL. *Dry.*

TALMADGE. Look at that moon. See the moon, Evie? You like the moon.

MARGERY. What did your parents do for a living?

MEL. My dad was a trapper, my momma mended blankets.

MARGERY. How interesting. Tell me more.

TALMADGE. Peanut?

MARGERY. Oh my. (*Picking up slingshot.*) What is this for?

MEL. Beanie shooter.

MARGERY. Beanie shooter. Mm. You shoot beans with it?

MEL. Hunt jack rabbits, prairie dogs. People.

TALMADGE. Did anyone see that TV show the other night where the cement mixer ran over a woman and another woman ran out on the road to save her little boy had a cerebral hemorrhage ended up with a brain transplant from the woman killed? By the cement mixer? I never saw the end. I've been wondering what happened when the husband came back from his trip and found his wife with another woman's brain in her. No one saw it?

MEL. Care to see me shoot?

MARGERY. I don't think so.

MEL. Roll down your window. We'll have us some fun.

MARGERY. You might hit a car.

MEL. Only if I want to.

TALMADGE. Hey! Well, what do you know? Big moment coming up everyone. The odometer is … creeping up to … ninety-nine thousand nine hundred and ninety-nine point eight …

MARGERY. All right. No. Sorry. It makes me a little nervous.

MEL. Thought you liked nervous.

TALMADGE. Ninety nine point nine …

MARGERY. Why do you say that?

TALMADGE. And … a …

MEL. Said you liked adventure.

———

TALMADGE. Half …

———

MARGERY. That's different.

———

TALMADGE. Hold on tight …

———

MEL. Asking a stranger for a ride.

———

TALMADGE. One … hundred … thousand miles! How 'bout that. Some car, huh? Yup, some car. Remember, Evie, that time at Myrtle Beach …

EVELYN. No.

TALMADGE. (*Brightly:*) You don't. Okay. (*Pause.*) Nice to hear your voice, sweetheart.

———

MARGERY. D.H. Lawrence, the writer, spent some time in Taos, didn't he?

MEL. Ol' Psyche, runs the La Fonda hotel, he's got all twenty-nine of D.H.'s paintings, mostly nudes. That's what they call 'em.

MARGERY. Nudes? Have you seen them? (*HE nods.*) Well, what do you think of them? Are they as sensuous as his writing?

MEL. I can't speak for his writing. Judging from his paintings I'd say the man was schizophrenic. Some folks have the cookies; some folks have the jar. (*Pause.*) That's what Psyche always says. 'Course he's Greek. You need to call home? Call your husband?

MARGERY. No.

———

TALMADGE. You know, Evie, there's going to be a lot of pressure at this tournament, more than you've ever had before. You might go all day and not catch a fish but you can't get upset, sweetheart. If you have confidence in that worm it'll work for you, sooner or later. Bear in mind, you got your Crawdad worm, your Strawberry Culprit worm, your Savage Do-Nothing, Gilraker and your Mann's Mannipulator.

EVELYN. One question.

TALMADGE. What is it, honey?

EVELYN. Are you remotely aware of what is going on in my mind right now? Are you?

TALMADGE. I am.

EVELYN. Then you know I'm typing.

TALMADGE. You're typing. Try to relax, honey. You're all tense.

EVELYN. Tense? Tense? Talmadge, the walls of my mind are riddled with holes. I pity the poor woman who wakes up with my brain as a transplant.

TALMADGE. What's Ramona fishing?

TEALE. She's asleep.

TALMADGE. Asleep? All year I've been hearing about the famous Ramona all time Bass'n Gal prize money winner world champion, won eleven boats in eight years, here she is in my car half an hour, she's asleep.

EVELYN. My car.

TALMADGE. Did you tell her we got to the airport nine hours early?

EVELYN. If I had been driving, as planned, Teale and I would have arrived forty-five minutes early.

TALMADGE. I'm not complaining, sweetheart. I liked the Albuquerque airport. Nice gift shop. Very pleasant. Do we have any soda left? Those peanuts made me thirsty.

EVELYN. You drank it all.

TALMADGE. I didn't drink it all.

EVELYN. You drank all the soda; hence, all the soda is gone.

TALMADGE. Mmm. Well, I know one thing. (*Sings in country western.*) "My honey heart is fishing the Bass'n Gal Classic and stands to win $30,000." Study those hills out there, Evie. Imagine them covered with water. It'll give you some idea of the structure on the bottom of Elephant Butte Reservoir.

TEALE. Hey, did we just pass a hospital sign?

EVELYN. Yes, we did, Teale. How's your asthma?

TEALE. Okay.

TALMADGE. Cripes, I shouldn't have eaten all that chili. Gave me terrible gas.

EVELYN. You think you're announcing something that everyone in this car isn't already acutely aware of?

MARGERY. I have to ask this. Don't think less of me for it. Are you a cowboy?

MEL. I'm a water dowser.

MARGERY. A water dowser? You're kidding. Really? Oo, that's wonderful. You're my very first water dower. That's where you use a stick, right? To find water?

MEL. Has to be green wood. Needs to be something in the tree really likes to find water.

MARGERY. Mm, a kindred spirit.

MEL. Chemistry.

MARGERY. Marvelous. How did you discover you have this gift?

MEL. Boy up in Colorado showed me how. First I'd practice over open water, wells, puddles, see how it felt. In later years, wouldn't work no more over open water.

MARGERY. No?

MEL. Guess I went on to bigger things.

MARGERY. It must be a highly valued skill where you're from. It being so ... dry.

MEL. You'd be surprised. Some denominations feel water witchin' is of the occult. My first wife, she went and read some book said dowsin' is devil's work. Witchcraft. She didn't want me doin' it no more. I stopped. Year later, started up again. Sure enough, she put my saddle out on the doorstep, bid me farewell, told me I was insensitive. To her feelings.

MARGERY. Did you marry again?

MEL. Married right now. To a world champion fisherwoman.

MARGERY. Ah.

MEL. She's got a gift for it, like mine. I find the water, she finds the fish. She's got her rod, I've got mine.

MARGERY. There was a woman on my plane on her way to a fishing tournament at Elephant Butte.

MEL. Is that right?

MARGERY. Uh-huh, she got on in Atlanta. She read my tea leaves from my tea bag. She told me romance was in the wings.

MEL. She wearing sunglasses, even indoors?

MARGERY. Yes she was.

MEL. Tell you anything about her husband?

MARGERY. Not that I recall.

MEL. Tell you anything about her boyfriend?

MARGERY. No. I did see someone pick her up at the airport. Right before I met you. He was wearing his pajamas. That's kind of romantic, don't you think? Whisking her off in his pajamas. Good Lord, look at that lightning.

MEL. Yep, I'm a family man, all right. I'm a *sensitive* man.

TEALE. (*Hits her chest and makes as loud a noise as possible.*) Hunh!!!

RAMONA. (*Wakes up, sits up.*) Jesus Christ almighty ...

EVELYN. Get back on the road!

TALMADGE. Teale, couldn't you give us some warning before you do that?

EVELYN. Get back on the road! We're entirely off the road!

MEL. Will you look at that. Pitiful.

MARGERY. Maybe you should pass them.

TEALE. Here's your beer, Ramona.

RAMONA. Thanks, Teale. Sorry folks, didn't mean to pass out on you all.

TALMADGE. Woo, look at that lightning.

RAMONA. Mn, lightning country down here. More lightning here than anywhere in the States.

TALMADGE. You didn't tell me that, honey.

RAMONA. Every year someone gets killed out on Elephant Butte reservoir. 'Course you're out there on that open water with that graphite fishing rod, may as well be holding a lightning rod.

TALMADGE. Oh, that's great. That's wonderful.

RAMONA. One time on my home lake there were two guys caught out in a storm. One of 'em had a life jacket on, the other was sitting on a cushion. They were hit by lighting. The fellow in the life jacket was killed. Other guy was castrated but he lived through it.

TALMADGE. Jesus.

RAMONA. After a few years his wife divorced him. Said he was just like a vegetable.

EVELYN. Well of course.

TALMADGE. What do you mean well of course?

RAMONA. Burst his balls right open.

TALMADGE. Ramona, we get the picture.

RAMONA. If you ever feel the back of your neck start tingling, or if the hair on your arm stands up, watch out. Lightning's coming. Could you roll your window down up there? I think something just died.

TALMADGE. Certainly, Ramona. I'd be more than happy to roll down the window.

RAMONA. Lord, Lord. Back in old New Mexico, the only state in the Union where you can still catch the plague.

TALMADGE. What plague?

RAMONA. What plague? I don't know what plague. *The* plague.

TALMADGE. How do you catch it?

RAMONA. I don't know how you catch the plague. How do you die in a plane crash?

TALMADGE. What did she say?

EVELYN. Teale tells me you used to live in New Mexico, Ramona.

RAMONA. Yup, lived up near Taos. Oh, those were grand times. My husband went schizophrenic on me. Tried to murder me.

EVELYN. Really?

RAMONA. I told him he was insensitive. He didn't like it.

TEALE. That's why he tried to murder you, just 'cause you told him he was insensitive?

RAMONA. Guess he'd heard it before. From his other wives.

TEALE. When d'you see him last?

RAMONA. Been a year at least. I expect I'll hear from him one of these days.

TALMADGE. Look at this bozo behind us, tailgating with his brights on. Why won't he just pass us?

MARGERY. I came to New Mexico twenty years ago for one week and I've wanted to come back ever since. It's odd the forces that pull us in certain directions, isn't it? Silly, really, why I should feel such a pull to come here.

MEL. Somethin' I'll never understand.

MARGERY. What, Mel?

MEL. How it is the same fish'll bite the same lure twice, three, four times, even after it's had its mouth all cut up. Bloody. Ripped to shreds.

TALMADGE. Ramona, I've been meaning to ask you something, have you tried out that new product Catch and Release yet?

EVELYN. *(Quietly.)* Talmadge.

RAMONA. Can't say as I have.

TALMADGE. It helps keep a fish alive through a stressful situation. See, when scales fall off a fish, there's a gland that produces a mucous coating to protect them; it soothes them, acts like a natural tranquilizer. The Catch and Release now, it stimulates that gland; helps you bring your fish back alive.

RAMONA. Anything that stimulates a gland can't be all bad. Evelyn, honey, this one's for you. Might lift your spirits some. After Adam and Eve made love for the first time, Eve went to the ocean to wash herself. God looked down, got all upset, flailed his arms, wrung his hands and cried, "Oh no, how'm I ever gonna get that smell out of the fish?"

EVELYN. That's a good one, Ramona. I like that.

TALMADGE. If I had told that joke, you'd be on me like fly paper.

TEALE. I don't get it.

RAMONA. (*Hitting her affectionately with her cap.*) Teale.

TALMADGE. Anyway, Ramona. I don't know if Evelyn told you but I work for Byrobie. We're small but we're growing fast with innovative new products like Catch and Release. We were wondering if you might be interested in posing in an advertisement for the Bass'n Gal magazine.

RAMONA. I'll think about it. I hear you're not fishing the Classic, Teale.

TEALE. I'm not. I'm just along to keep Evelyn company, introduce you'all. Help out with the driving.

RAMONA. What's Talmadge doing?

TEALE. Talmadge got in the car at the last second, just as we were pulling out the driveway. That's why your door's all banged up. He flung it into a tree, piling in.

RAMONA. Huh. Could you keep your window down up there? Whatever it was just died is going through some more of that bad stress.

MARGERY. Driving at night can be so hypnotic, don't you think? As if the road were driving us. Funny, fate. Perfect strangers sharing a journey, perhaps the three most important hours of our life. What is it that's pulling us toward it, beyond the headlights out there. Some remnant from our past, some piece of ourselves.

MEL. You sound like that fellow from the Twilight Zone.

MARGERY. I know I probably sound ridiculous. It just always seems curious to me what it is that makes people chose the disastrous courses they do. I mean, look at me right now. What was it that made me ask you for a ride at the airport? You could be a mass murderer for all I know. Isn't it odd how you can open up to a total stranger, share things you would never tell anyone else, knowing you'll never see that person again. I feel very close to you right now. Ask me something personal, I'll tell you anything. Go ahead. Let me give you something of value, something intimate.

MEL. I don't know, m'am ...

MARGERY. Please. Go ahead, you'll be doing me a kindness.

MEL. Intimate. Physical?

MARGERY. I know what I'll tell you, I've never told this to anyone before. Ha, I can't believe I'm telling you this. When I was twelve, my Aunt Claire took it upon herself to inform me of the facts of life. I don't know why but she began the conversation by telling me about her heart murmur. For some reason I mixed it all up and for the longest time I thought that an orgasm was something that happened in your heart. Isn't that a remarkable idea? Isn't it? You can imagine how confused I was later on. (*Laughs. Pause.*) There, now you know something about me that no one else knows. (*Pause.*) Don't you think it's actually quite poetic? An involuntary stirring in the heart? (*Pause.*) So. (*Pause.*) Well. (*Pause.*) Is there any more Coca-cola left? My throat's gone dry.

MEL. It's all gone.

MARGERY. Well, what do you think?

MEL. About what?

MARGERY. My story. About my aunt.

MEL. I don't.

MARGERY. Oh. (*Pause.*) My, the sky is certainly enormous out here, isn't it?

MEL. What am I supposed to think?

MARGERY. You aren't supposed to think anything. I just thought you might have a response and if you did, you might share it with me.

—

RAMONA. Play us another tune, Teale.

(*The pace of the tune she picks should build, enhancing the scene's pace, in a minor key.*)

—

MEL. You know, m'am, you might should be a little more careful about selecting your adventures.

MARGERY. What do you mean?

MEL. Getting into a car with a perfect stranger. Might be some day you get into the wrong car.

MARGERY. Do you think we could stop at this diner up here? My husband is expecting me to call him.

MEL. You said he wasn't.

MARGERY. Beg your pardon?

MEL. You said he wasn't.

MARGERY. Look, I'm beginning to feel quite uncomfortable.

MEL. Roll down your window, m'am.

MARGERY. Stop the car right now.

MEL. Your window. Roll it down now.

MARGERY. You're speeding up.

MEL. (*Has slingshot out.*) Just wanna pass this car.

MARGERY. Oh God, don't shoot me!

MEL. Don't move, m'am. (*Fires past her.*) Bingo!

TALMADGE. Ow!

EVELYN. What happened?

TALMADGE. Something hit me. Ow, hurts.

EVELYN. Are you all right?

RAMONA. What was it?

TALMADGE. I don't know. A rock.

RAMONA. Was that an old pick-up that just passed us?

EVELYN. Do you want to stop?

TALMADGE. I knew I didn't want you coming out here, Evelyn. I knew it.

EVELYN. Pull over, honey. We'll get out the first aid kit.

TALMADGE. Evie, I want you to be very careful while you're in New Mexico. Very careful. Promise me you will be. Promise.

EVELYN. I will.

Scene 3

Later that night. A campground on Elephant Butte Reservoir. EVELYN, RAMONA and TEALE enter carrying two lit lanterns, sleeping bags, night bags. THEY unroll their sleeping bags, laying them out in a semi-circle so they can sit on them during the scene as THEY prepare for bed. RAMONA has a couple of rods and her tackle box with her. SHE checks her lines, sharpens her hooks, etc.

TEALE. (*Plays harmonica, starts coughing; hits chest three times with her fist in a fighting spirit.*) Hunh! Hunh!! Hunh!!

RAMONA. Christ almighty. I hope nothing big, hairy and diseased is in heat around here. Why do you do that, Teale?

EVELYN. (*Has a topo map of Elephant Butte in front of her; SHE is sniffing a little jar from Ramona's tacklebox.*) This smells like licorice.

RAMONA. Fish perfume. You spray it on a lure, makes a fish more aggressive. Gives you a better crack at catching a bigger fish. The older the fish, the better his sense of smell.

TEALE. Hey, somebody's watching us.

RAMONA. This is your first Classic, Evelyn, isn't it?

EVELYN. Yes it is and now I know what Classic butterflies are. I'm scared to death I'll go out there and I won't catch anything.

RAMONA. The pressure will be hard, hard as a booger. But I tell you what ... if you aren't catching anything, just sit back and enjoy the scenery. Elephant Butte Reservoir is the most beautiful lake I've ever seen. It's got every type of structure you could want to fish; shallow or deep and the water is clear, gin clear.

TEALE. Somebody just moved.

EVELYN. Where?

TEALE. Behind that cottonwood.

RAMONA. Some old dust devil. They got a new rule this year you got to have a kill switch, a little cord that's attached to your body. If you fall over, the motor cuts out.

EVELYN. I heard. I know a woman who clips it to her bra. What time are we supposed to check in at the marina tomorrow?

RAMONA. Should be there by five-thirty to check out our boats. It's just ten minutes up the road.

EVELYN. (*Setting her alarm clock.*) Maybe we should aim for five-fifteen.

TEALE. I know a woman keeps her worms in her bra. She does.

RAMONA. Teale, what happened to you this year? You must have fished the last five Classics. How come you didn't qualify?

TEALE. Bad year.

RAMONA. What happened?

TEALE. When?

RAMONA. This year.

TEALE. Huh?

RAMONA. What happened to you that was so bad you didn't qualify for the Classic.

TEALE. Oh.

RAMONA. (*Waits to hear what.*) That bad, huh? Well, I'm sorry. What happened to the Jack Daniels?

TEALE. Personal stuff.

EVELYN. It's over here, Ramona.

(SHE hands the bottle to RAMONA who takes a swig and hands it back; EVELYN drinks from it heavily throughout the scene.)

TEALE. Randy, my husband, managed to knock himself into the septic tank with the backhoe, don't ask me how. He was cleaning it out ended up plunging wrist first into the tank. Shattered his arm in a million places like a windshield. Next thing you know, I'm working a double shift and Randy is having an affair with the night waitress at Mr. Donut.

EVELYN. Right on the premises. Can you imagine the gall?

RAMONA. At Mr. Donut?

EVELYN. One time she found blackberry filling all over his credit cards, didn't you Teale?

TEALE. 'Course, everyone in town's been in *her*.

RAMONA. Don't feel bad, honey. Men just feel inadequate. They don't know the art of making love; they just know the art of screwing and that's not an art. Most of them are only five minutes in the act anyway. Evelyn, these rice crispie bars are divine.

EVELYN. Thank you, Ramona. I took the recipe right off the box.

TEALE. (*Wistfully.*) Randy's pretty good.

RAMONA. Listen, they're all just out looking for their mothers, anyway. Someone to take care of them. Only they want pretty young mothers. It's incestuous, really it is.

TEALE. He was awful nice to sleep next to. Soft.

RAMONA. Was?

TEALE. Haven't seen him in five months. Next thing I know he'll probably show up in a Mr. Donut commercial.

EVELYN. You'll meet somebody else soon, Teale. All men feel nice in the dark. When you get right down to it, it really doesn't matter who you're sleeping next to; given he's asleep. What kind of lure is this?

RAMONA. It's a chartreuse gold flake skirted pro-bushwacker with a sampo ballbearing swivel and a stinger hook. From Bomber Bait.

EVELYN. Pretty. Teale says you like the Zara Spook.

RAMONA. Yeah, I do. I like it 'cause it pisses the fish off. Doesn't try to tempt him or nothing, act sultry; just riles him. What are you fishing tomorrow?

EVELYN. Spinnerbait.

RAMONA. Sounds good. You ever try casting underhanded?

EVELYN. Underhanded? No.

RAMONA. If we get a chance this weekend, I'll show you.

EVELYN. Thank you.

RAMONA. Underhanded cast takes two seconds less than overhanded. Saves a lot of air time. You can develop more speed, make more casts, cover more water.

EVELYN. Thank you.

RAMONA. My pleasure.

TEALE. The worst of it, Ramona, is now I've got asthma. I know it's partly mental.

RAMONA. Mental's bad. I've been there before.

TEALE. I've been to the emergency room three times this fall, couldn't get my breath. Lou, the driver for the first responders, seen me so often he knows my place and date of birth by heart.

RAMONA. Maybe he's interested in you.

TEALE. Lou? You think so?

RAMONA. Could be.

TEALE. Lou? No. Really? Nah.

EVELYN. I'm doing this mental thing it's got me just about ready to move out of my mind.

RAMONA. What's that?

TEALE. (*Grabs toilet paper.*) I'm taking a whiz. (*Exits with lantern.*)

EVELYN. I type everything I read or hear. Billboards, road signs, I type what people are saying. I'll zip ahead and finish off their sentences.

RAMONA. What do you mean type?

EVELYN. Type, on a keyboard, in my mind, in my fingers. I'll type jingles on the radio, the hit parade, my own thoughts. I'll type them backwards, use the fingers on the opposite hands? Or mirror image. Say it's a word like "fishing." Instead of typing the f with this finger (*Raises index finger.*) I'll type it with this finger (*Raises little finger.*) See this finger's (*Touches index.*) the opposite of this finger (*Touches little finger.*) and this finger's (*Touches middle finger.*) the opposite of this finger (*Touches fourth finger.*). So "fishing" instead of this (*Types.*) is this (*Types.*) I can do it with both hands, mirror-image, or backwards mirror image. I can type the word itself backwards, backward mirror-image. I do it all the time, whether I'm frying or fending off Talmadge. All up and down my arms, from here (*Points to head.*) to here (*Wiggles fingertips.*), constant traffic. Steady flow. All day long. Go figure.

RAMONA. Jesus.

EVELYN. "Timil deeps"; that's "speed limit" backwards. (*Spells while typing.*) "T i m i l. D e e p s." Now I'm typing it backwards forwards. Now, here it is backwards mirror image? See?

RAMONA. You know, you could probably read the Satanic Bible in the original. It's written backwards upside down. That's how the devil wrote.

EVELYN. Really?

RAMONA. Uh-huh. Whenever witches write to the devil they always write backwards upside down.

EVELYN. I believe it. It's hell, let me tell you.

RAMONA. Evelyn, honey, you better slow down on that bottle. How long has this been going on?

(TEALE enters and sits on her sleeping bag.)

EVELYN. I used to do it a long time ago, in my later teenage years. I started the summer I was a telephone operator for western union, got up to one hundred and two words a minute. When I went to junior college I had to drop out because I couldn't hear what the teachers were saying, my mind was too besieged.

RAMONA. You went to junior college?

EVELYN. Yes I did for about two months till I had to drop out, and do you think I got any tuition refund? "Could I please have my eight hundred dollars back?" Quote why unquote. "Oh, I'm typing in my mind." I know it has to do with being tense, I know it does. I was a very tense teenager.

RAMONA. You tense now, Evelyn?

EVELYN. Apparently.

RAMONA. Why?

EVELYN. I'm not really sure.

TEALE. I'm back.

EVELYN. Talmadge is really pushing for us to get married but that's nothing new. My boss wants to open up another Men's World on the other side of Clarkesburg.

RAMONA. Men's world?

EVELYN. It's a health club. For men.

RAMONA. I figured.

EVELYN. I'm secretary to the owner. He wants to open up another branch and appoint me office manager.

RAMONA. Office manager sounds pretty good.

EVELYN. Mm. 'Course it would mean going full time and Talmadge isn't too wild about that. I'm not really sure I have the confidence to do it anyway. I haven't been feeling overly confident lately.

RAMONA. Too bad my grandmother's dead. She might could of helped you with your typing.

EVELYN. (*Still drinking.*) How?

RAMONA. She had all the remedies, remedies for anything. I remember my dad used to get these big heavy warts on his hands. They'd get all black with a kind of callous on them and then they'd branch out into little warts and they'd grow big. They were really ugly.

TEALE. Like plantar's warts?

RAMONA. No, Teale. Those are on your feet. Well, being a plumber, he used to snag them all the time. Maybe he'd be threading a pipe, or crawling up under the house, and he'd snag his warts and pull them halfway off and they'd grow back even bigger. In those days the doctors could scoop them with those metal things? But they didn't know how to kill them. It's a kind of disease. Well, Francis would take an old dish rag—they'd sour sometimes in the summer—get all mouldy and stink, just flopped up on the faucet. She'd wait for the moon to be just right and then she'd take that nasty dish rag and rub it all over those hands. She'd say something, I don't know what it was, in another language, and then she'd go out and bury the rag someplace special in the yard. She didn't want anyone watching to see where. My dad would go to sleep and when he'd wake up the next morning, his hands were clean. The warts were gone.

(EVELYN gasps.)

TEALE. What happened to the rag?

RAMONA. She was quite a woman. Taught me how to fish. Lake Fork, East Texas.

TEALE. What happened to the rag?

RAMONA. I don't know, Teale.

EVELYN. (*Quite drunk.*) It just shows to go you. Our mind has a mind of its own that isn't even ours. Your liver is making bile this very instant and you aren't even lifting a finger. You have no say in the matter.

RAMONA. Pass me another of those rice crispie bars.

EVELYN. Your body could be planning a whole row of warts right now. Right across your face. Like a zipper. And you would be the last to know.

RAMONA. These are so good.

EVELYN. You know that TV show "It's *Your* Life?" Ha! That's a laugh and a half.

TEALE. I wonder what your grandmother would give for asthma.

RAMONA. Most likely same thing she'd give Evelyn for her typing. You're both doing different steps to the same dance. Just trying to make some sense, get some control. It's like wallpapering the world with your own familiar pattern; everyone does it. Everyone's their own universe. What are you staring at, Teale?

TEALE. You should be on the Phil Donahue show, Ramona. You'd be awesome on a panel. You know there've been times I've laid down my rod and just watched you fish. Captures the eye.

EVELYN. My next door neighbor, Eunice? Her eldest girl, Felicity, was taking modern dance with a friend, a very pretty girl, in her early teens. Well. The friend missed several weeks of dance class and when she did finally return, she had all these little odd scars all around her nose up under her eyes. The explanation was that this moth or some other type of insect had flown up her nose and lodged in her sinus cavity and apparently laid eggs. One night at the dinner table they *hatched* and the sensation, whatever it was, was so awful that she started to gouge at her face with her hands, and when that didn't relieve it she picked up a fork and began to stab at her face.

TEALE. Gee.

RAMONA. You got to get that typewriter out of your mind, girl. Drowning it ain't the way to get it out. (*Takes the bottle.*)

EVELYN. (*Walks downstage and looks up over audience.*) How come they call it Elephant Butte? It doesn't look like a elephant.

RAMONA. (*Joining her.*) Yeah, it does. Look, there's the head …

EVELYN. Where?

RAMONA. Up there.

EVELYN. Where?

(TEALE joins them.)

RAMONA. In between the ears. See?

EVELYN. No.

RAMONA. There's the trunk.

EVELYN. Am I mad?

RAMONA. It's a old elephant, a hundred thousand centuries old, all dried out inside. Poor guy must be thirsty staring out at all that water.

EVELYN. Where are his lips?

RAMONA. He walked through all that sand and time just to get to that big ol' watering hole, and right when he got there his insides seized up, turned to stone. The dry wet dreams of Elephant Butte.

EVELYN. Hey … I can *see* … I can see one … vertical … hair, moving. One vertical moving elephant hair. It's walking from one elephant ear … to the other.

TEALE. Yeah.

RAMONA. Well shit howdy. There he is.

EVELYN. (*Using her fingers to crawl up and down Teale's leg.*) Why did the ant crawl up the elephant's leg and then come crawling all the way back down and then crawl all the way on back up again and then crawl all the way back down again and then crawl all the way back up again?

TEALE. Why?

EVELYN. 'Cause he was pissed off. (*Dissolves in laughter around Teale's feet.*)

TALMADGE. (*Wearing a band-aid on his face from the shot, new khaki trousers and a New Mexico sweatshirt.*) Hi everyone. I know, I know. I was just driving by. I really did leave you, Evelyn ... just like I promised ... I left you...

(*RAMONA walks away to give them some space. TEALE stays near Evelyn and listens intently to Talmadge.*)

TALMADGE. Evelyn, I don't think you should sleep here tonight. I don't, I really don't. This is just not a good place for you sleep, out here, on the ground. Mexico is just down the road. In my gut, Evelyn, I have bad feelings about this whole idea. So. Why don't you come with me, we'll get a motel room, I'll drive you to the marina early in the morning. Okay? (*HE takes her hand to pull her up and leave.*)

EVELYN. (*Slapping his hand.*) No!

TALMADGE. Evelyn. Be reasonable. There are scorpions. There are snakes, flying rocks. Strange natives, I've met a few. It's very dark.

EVELYN. No!

TALMADGE. Evelyn. Are you okay? You look a little off kilter; it's a little alarming. Sweetheart, the man at the marina says there's a storm system coming through, a big storm and quite frankly I'm not wild about the idea of you fishing out on that lake tomorrow given the high incidence of lightning in this area. So, we'll spend the night together...

EVELYN. No!

TALMADGE. Evelyn. Okay. Okay. (*HE stares at Teale and finally stirs her to move away.*) I didn't want to tell you this now, I did not. I wanted it to be special, some special circumstance, but sweetheart, you're pregnant. You are. Pregnant. Surprise! Isn't it wonderful? So, now, I'm sure you'll agree, we neither of us would want our baby spending the night out here, in a sleeping bag ...

(There is a loud GUNSHOT. TALMADGE screams and falls.)

EVELYN. (*Going to him.*) Talmadge! Are you hurt?

TALMADGE. Yes!

RAMONA. (*Looking up at the butte.*) Jesus H. Christ!

EVELYN. Where? Where are you hurt?

TALMADGE. (*On the ground.*) I'm hurt everywhere, Evelyn. (*HE grabs her by the arm.*) We're getting the fuck out of here.

(Another GUNSHOT. TALMADGE hauls EVELYN off and TEALE follows them.)

RAMONA. (*Fired up and having a good time raging out front towards the butte.*) God dammit, Mel! You promised me you'd never fire at me again. You promised, you gave me your word, got down on your knees, kissed your Bible, swore up and down the Virgin Mary, Mel Graves you *vowed* you'd never ever take another shot at me. Now, you cut it out, I mean it, God dammit. (*Points into the darkness.*) Don't you ever *ever* shoot at me again. You hear me? Ever! Never! I am sick of it. Sick of it! I have had it with your bullets! (*Turns away and laughs to herself.*) Sons of bitches. It's enough to give a dog's rectum heartburn.

(*Pause. TEALE creeps on.*)

TEALE. (*Whispers loud.*) Ramona!

RAMONA. Huh?

TEALE. C'mon.

RAMONA. What?

TEALE. Come on.

RAMONA. I'm not coming on anywheres except right here. Tell you what, I'm going to sleep right now. I got a big day tomorrow. I gotta catch some *big* lunkers win me $30,000 that's what. You come on, Teale, he won't fire any more. He's spent.

TEALE. You sure?

RAMONA. He knows he fires at me again tonight he's dead meat. Dead meat! Go to bed, Teale.

TEALE. (*Crosses over to her sleeping bag, ducking down.*) Do you know him?

RAMONA. Yeah.

TEALE. Who is it?

RAMONA. My husband.

TEALE. I didn't know you still had a husband.

RAMONA. I do.

TEALE. Why's he shooting you at you?

RAMONA. Ah, he's got himself into a bad habit.

TEALE. Why does he do it?

RAMONA. Why? You ever had a conversation with a hunter, Teale?

TEALE. Yeah.

RAMONA. Then you know why it is a man likes to shoot. Then you know that when a hunter has gone and shot himself a deer, he wants it to be the most beautiful lovely deer in all the forest. The more beautiful the deer, the sweeter he feels sitting there in the woods holding that dead deer's head in his lap, stroking it, the more in love he is. It's a sexual thing, Teale.

TEALE. Huh?

RAMONA. Killing is as close as a man can get to giving birth. It's as close as he can get to putting his hands on the life force.

TEALE. Gee.

RAMONA. Putting his hands *on* it, feeling it up inside his teeth, and most important, directing it, being in charge for once in his poor pitiful life instead of getting battered around. You don't have any dental floss, do you?

TEALE. No. Sorry. Got some light test fishing line. Eight pound?

RAMONA. Mm, cut me a piece, would you?

TEALE. Does he really want to kill you?

RAMONA. If he knew he could do it again, he would. He doesn't want it to be over. Best he can do is just hover around it.

TEALE. Did you know he was gonna come?

RAMONA. Yeah, I knew. I invited him.

TEALE. You invited him?

RAMONA. Sent him a Zara Spook, put a little coconut oil on it. That was invitation enough. He didn't put up one bit of a fight, did he? You just got to know how to work those underground currents.

TEALE. I don't understand.

RAMONA. Hate. Then too, it's a sexual thing.

TEALE. Oh. (*TEALE gets into her sleeping bag.*)

RAMONA. See, love is hard to get over, but hate is much harder; takes a lot longer. When you do finally let go of hate you are stranded in a loneliness that is deathly still. It can be devastating.

TEALE. He hates you?

RAMONA. Me and three wives before me.

TEALE. But you don't hate him. Not if you wanted him to come.

RAMONA. Mm, hard to call it. Way I figure it is, feelings are kind of like matter. You can't destroy them; they just take a different form.

TEALE. You think he's still out there?

RAMONA. I know it. He's up on that big stone elephant right now, sitting up on the head, riding that stone working up a breeze in his mind. Pew, this sleeping bag smells of cat piss. Tell you what, Teale, I don't know who's got the bigger thirst ... that big stone elephant or that little stone man.

(Pause.)

TEALE. What were you saying before, Ramona, about my asthma and wallpapering the world?

RAMONA. Huh?

TEALE. Something about control?

RAMONA. I don't remember.

TEALE. Everyone's one familiar pattern?

RAMONA. (*Staring up at butte.*) Oh yeah, put your own crazy pattern up all around you. Only trouble is when you shut the world out, you shut yourself in.

TEALE. You think asthma's a pattern?

RAMONA. Could be. Way I look at disease, a person suffers enough pain in the world, after a while they get to making their own pain. Body figures if it's gonna be a victim, might as well be its own. (*Laughs.*) First time ever heard a man tell a woman she's pregnant. Funny thing is, I believe him.

(TEALE covers face with arm.)

RAMONA. Teale. Teale? You crying?

TEALE. No. Yeah.

RAMONA. What's wrong?

TEALE. Nothing.

RAMONA. You don't fall in the victim category, honey. You'll get over it. You sleep well now.

TEALE. Feel like I'm in jail.

(RAMONA puts out lantern; lies down. Another GUNSHOT. BOTH sit upright.)

TEALE. (*Fearful.*) Geez!

RAMONA. God dammit!

BLACKOUT

ACT II

Scene 1

The next morning. EVELYN and TEALE are out on the lake in a boat. EVELYN stands in the back of the boat and casts fervently over and over, watching the lure come in as SHE reels it towards the boat. TEALE sits in front of her, looking around through her binoculars. There is a little SPLASH.

EVELYN. (*Turning around.*) I wish those ducks wouldn't do that. Every time I hear them I think it's a fish. Teale, what time is it?

TEALE. Eleven thirty-four.

EVELYN. I would feel significantly better if I had a keeper in the well. Could you get me a bite of something?

TEALE. Sure. (*Gets food and a soda with a straw and stands behind her, feeding her.*) You've developed a real nice retrieve, Evelyn; that minnow looks hurt.

EVELYN. Thank you.

TEALE. Mm, I think that's Virginia's boat.

EVELYN. She better not put her anchor down on me.

TEALE. She won't. Can't fish within fifty yards. Hey Virginia! (*Holds up soda and waves it at her.*) This morning at the marina she brought a pot of coffee over half real coffee half decaf poured in together. Said that way everyone could drink it. Ramona says Virginia couldn't pour piss out of a boot if the instructions were written on the heel. (*Pause.*) What does that mean?

EVELYN. I don't relish fishing in a crowd.

TEALE. Don't worry, she's going. (*TEALE goes back to the front and sits down.*) Sure feels funny. Not fishin'. Looks like that storm is coming in after all. If it comes in right, it'll make your fish more active. Did you get any sleep last night, Evelyn?

EVELYN. If you call passing out on some stranger's tarp and being unconscious for a while sleep, then I had some.

TEALE. I never saw you drunk like that before.

EVELYN. Yes you did too.

TEALE. No I did not.

EVELYN. You saw me drunk that time after Helen's graduation party we all went to The Flying Pig for barbecue. Remember? Talmadge proposed to me in the vestibule? Grady's pants caught on fire?

TEALE. Oh yeah. You were drunk. Where's Talmadge now?

EVELYN. Talmadge is right now in the car, heading west. He's planning to turn around at three and pick us up at the banquet.

TEALE. You gonna marry him now?

EVELYN. Teale. I'm in the Classic.

TEALE. You want some more sun screen on your nose? It's getting kind of pink.

EVELYN. (*Nods.*) Could you put your foot on the trolling motor and angle us a little that way?

TEALE. Sure. (*Standing in front of her, TEALE reaches back with her foot to the trolling motor while applying sunscreen to Evelyn's nose.*) Did you know that was Ramona's husband last night, shooting at us?

EVELYN. No.

TEALE. It was too.

EVELYN. I didn't know Ramona still had a husband.

TEALE. She does.

EVELYN. I hate to think what Ramona thinks of me now. Getting drunk before a tournament. Teale, something just flew into my eye. Do you think you could get it out?

TEALE. Sure.

EVELYN. Do you see anything?

TEALE. I see a fleck.

EVELYN. A fleck?

TEALE. Look up.

EVELYN. Could you not use your fingernail, Teale? Don't you have a tissue?

TEALE. Almost got it. Maybe you should stop fishing for a sec.

EVELYN. I can't stop fishing for a sec. I can't stop fishing for an instant. I can't afford it.

TEALE. Got it.

EVELYN. Thank you.

TEALE. (*Studying it.*) It's a bug. No, it's not. Yes, it is too. No ...

EVELYN. Teale, I need to catch a respectable fish. You don't know how much it means to me. I have no business being here.

TEALE. (*Sitting down.*) Put your mind into your lure. Imagine you're that wounded minnow, flittin' along the surface. That's what I do with surface lures. Makes a big difference. When I'm fishin' plugs or jigs or crank bait, I'll put my mind down in the fish, pretend I'm the old lunker down there in the dark.

EVELYN. Okay. Would you take a Ph reading?

TEALE. Sure (*Gets meter; dunks it.*)

EVELYN. It should be going up.

TEALE. It is. Seven point six.

EVELYN. Should make for good top water action, shouldn't it?

TEALE. Should. (*Puts meter back in tackle box.*) Hey, there's a note in here.

EVELYN. A note?

TEALE. It's from Talmadge. With a little valentine candy heart. (*Reading candy.*) "Oh baby." Want me to read you the note?

EVELYN. Do me a favor, Teale. Kindly destroy the note and eat the candy.

TEALE. Kind of nice he loves you so much. (*Takes out binoculars.*) Sure is pretty. Those seed pods hanging on those brushes look like dried yellow minnows. I remember long time ago, 'bout fifteen years back when Randy and I first went fishing, he'd go out in the boat with his friends and I'd stay home on the bank. He didn't realize I would like to have went in the boat. All the locals they knew me. They'd say if Teale can't catch them, no use puttin' in. I used to fish rip rap. I guess he thought I liked it fishin' from tho bank.

EVELYN. You think I'm right throwing a quarter-ounce?

TEALE. You considering a three-eighth?

EVELYN. Yeah.

TEALE. I wouldn't go up. You know Mary works at the marina? Last year her husband died, they cremated him, put his ashes up there you can see a little cross way up on that butte. (*Pause.*) You know a good test to tell if you you're really in love with someone? Just imagine being buried next to him. Forever. Gee, that storm is coming in. Hey!

EVELYN. What?

TEALE. Someone's on the shore there, waving his arms. Looks like … it is. It's Talmadge.

EVELYN. You're kidding.

TEALE. It's him. No mistaking Talmadge.

EVELYN. We're leaving.

TEALE. I hope no one starts shooting at us.

EVELYN. We're going up to Willow Canyon. Darn it all. There's something down there.

TEALE. Uh-oh.

EVELYN. What's he doing now?

TEALE. I don't have my inhaler. For my asthma? I'm supposed to do it every four hours and four hours is up.

EVELYN. Where is it?

TEALE. Must of left it at the marina.

EVELYN. I've got your pills here, your theophylline.

TEALE. It's the inhaler I need.

EVELYN. Should I take you back? I better.

TEALE. No, no. I'm fine. Forget it. It's okay.

EVELYN. Teale …

TEALE. Just keep fishing. I'll be all right.

EVELYN. We've got another four hours to go. Will you be okay?

TEALE. Yeah, I'll be fine.

EVELYN. Have you ever not used your inhaler for that length of time?

TEALE. Sure.

EVELYN. Sure?

TEALE. Sure.

EVELYN. One more cast.

TEALE. (*Softly.*) No.

EVELYN. Just look at him. He has zero faith in me, Teale. Zero. Wait.

TEALE. Got a snag?

EVELYN. Doesn't feel like a snag.

TEALE. Set the hook. Set the hook!

EVELYN. I set it, I set it! Oh God, it's a … this is a big … Teale ... oh gosh … I'm not kidding … whew! … it's big …

TEALE. Careful.

EVELYN. Don't get off. Please don't get off.

TEALE. I got the net ready.

EVELYN. You got the net ready?

TEALE. I got the net ready.

EVELYN. Don't get off. Don't get off. Please don't get off. Whoo! Did you see him?

TEALE. Yeah. He's big.

EVELYN. I told you. You got the net ready?

TEALE. Got it.

TEALE and EVELYN. (*Together:*) Here he comes.

(LIGHTS start to fade. Her fishing line can be taut now, making the rod bend, but the fish shouldn't appear.)

EVELYN. Oh God, thank you, thank you, thank you. I really appreciate this.

TEALE. You're grinnin' like a skunk eatin' bumblebees.

EVELYN. I did it.

TEALE. That's some beauty.
EVELYN. I did it!

(LIGHTS out. TALMADGE'S VOICE is heard shouting. EVELYN and TEALE exit.)

Scene 2

On the lake shore. It is best if the lake is played out front.

TALMADGE. (*Running up and down the shore, shouting, waving his arms.*) Evelyn! Evie! Get off the water! Lightning! It's gonna rain, sweetheart, it's gonna pour! Evie, look up at the sky! Look up at the sky! God forbid she should once in her life look up at the sky. There's gonna be lightning! There is. It's storming up! Evie! Go back to the marina! Oh God, please make her go back. Get rid of your pole! Throw it out of the boat, it acts as a lightning rod, give it to Teale! Why did I ever get her that pole in the first place, why didn't I just get her that home entertainment center for her VCR I could have got it with my green stamps go back to the marina!

(HE runs and bumps into MEL who has entered, carrying a rifle over his shoulder. TALMADGE is startled.)

TALMADGE. I'm sorry. I didn't see you.
MEL. What's your trouble, boy?
TALMADGE. (*Trying to gain composure.*) Nothing. Just someone out there on the water.

MEL. There's someone out there on the water?

TALMADGE. Yes.

MEL. Is that right?

TALMADGE. Uh-huh. They're fishing. She's fishing. There's a tournament, a fishing tournament.

MEL. (*Nods.*) Out on the water.

TALMADGE. Uh-huh.

MEL. How 'bout that.

TALMADGE. Actually, my wife is out in it, in the tournament, on the water, and I'm a little concerned.

MEL. Your wife? That gal you're with is your wife?

TALMADGE. Well, no, not really, not yet, she's just my girlfriend now. Look! The little hairs on my arm are standing up.

MEL. They stand up every time you lie?

TALMADGE. They stand up when it's going to lightning. Have lightning. Be lightning.

MEL. That's why you're concerned about her. Your girlfriend.

TALMADGE. (*Tries to stay composed.*) Yes, I am. I am. Concerned (*Long pause.*) Nice rifle. (*Pause.*) How 'bout those Oakland Raiders, huh? Is that Joe Montana something else? (*No response.*) Well, I guess I better be going. (*Moves toward him to leave.*) Maybe I'll catch her in the next canyon.

MEL. (*Steps in front of him.*) What's your hurry, boy. Can't get out of life alive.

TALMADGE. See, she's pregnant. She doesn't really realize it yet, but she is.

MEL. She's pregnant?

TALMADGE. Yeah.

MEL. You got her pregnant?

TALMADGE. Yup. She's late. She's over two weeks late. Her mind's been on her fishing.

MEL. (*Grabs him by the collar.*) You lying again?

TALMADGE. I beg your pardon?

MEL. You got my wife pregnant? (*Raises rifle.*)

TALMADGE. Your wife? Oh no, not your wife. I wouldn't dream of getting your wife pregnant. Look. (*HE moves rifle away toward lake.*) Could you please fire your gun a couple times to try to get her attention over here? I haven't been able to get her attention. (*A loud THUNDER clap; TALMADGE loses control.*) Evie! Evelyn!

MEL. Evelyn? Who's Evelyn?

TALMADGE. Evelyn, get off the water!

MEL. Aren't you with Ramona?

TALMADGE. Please get off the water!

MEL. You picked Ramona up at the airport. I saw her get into your car with you.

TALMADGE. (*Elated.*) They're leaving! Thank God! Goddammit it, that's not the way to the marina. That's the complete opposite direction. Look, they're going the complete wrong direction. The other way! Evie, turn around! Turn around, honey! (*Another THUNDER clap.*) Evie! (*Grabs Mel and cries.*) Oh, Jesus I don't want her to die. Evie …

MEL. (*Inadvertently comforting him.*) She'll be all right.

TALMADGE. Every year someone dies on this lake from lightning.

MEL. No they don't.

TALMADGE. Yes they do.

MEL. Who told you that?

TALMADGE. Ramona. She's a friend of my wife. I mean my girlfriend.

MEL. You can't believe her.

TALMADGE. She's the world champion.

MEL. You can't believe her.

TALMADGE. Do you know her? You know Ramona? Does she lie?

MEL. Yeah, I know her. Look, pal, pull yourself together. Storms come through here all the time, no one gets hurt. Trust me, she'll be all right.

TALMADGE. I'll try. I'll try to trust you. Are you from this area? Do you know this area? You know people don't get hit by lightning every year?

MEL. Yeah. (*Starts to leave.*)

TALMADGE. All right. Thank you so much. You're a sensitive man.

MEL. (*Stops in his tracks.*) What did you call me?

TALMADGE. Uh … sorry, I didn't mean to offend you. Someone as tough as you … with a rifle and all.

MEL. You said I was sensitive.

TALMADGE. I did. My apologies. You aren't sensitive.

MEL. I'm not?

TALMADGE. Are you?

MEL. You said I was.

TALMADGE. Is that all right?

MEL. Yeah. It's all right.

TALMADGE. Good.

MEL. I am a sensitive man.

TALMADGE. You know, you really are. You just might be the most sensitive man I've ever met.

MEL. Thank you. (*Tears up, overwhelmed. Pause.*) You ever been to New Mexico before?

TALMADGE. No.

MEL. How do you like it?

TALMADGE. (*Smiles; still ingratiating.*) I don't.

MEL. (*Hasn't heard.*) Uh-huh.

(Long awkward pause. BOTH MEN face forward, out towards the lake. When Talmadge asks him the following, it is still with some caution and fear of this New Mexico native with a rifle.)

TALMADGE. You didn't happen to see that TV show last week where the woman was killed by a cement mixer? The other woman who saved her boy, knocked him out of the way, had a cerebral hemorrhage, got her brain as a transplant? And then the husband came back?

MEL. No, I didn't catch that one.

TALMADGE. Mm. I missed the end. I was just wondering if the dead woman's personality came with her brain, or if the woman with the body was who that person was. (*Pause.*) If the person was the brain or the body. If it was the brain I just wondered how the husband felt to come home and find someone else in his wife.

MEL. In his wife?

TALMADGE. But maybe it wasn't. Maybe it was just his wife who stayed in his wife; she just took over the new brain.

MEL. Hunh.

(Long pause.)

MEL. You know, if I was to take a forked willow branch and hold it over that water right now it wouldn't budge.

TALMADGE. Really?

MEL. Only works on water underground.

TALMADGE. Huh.

MEL. Kind of like love. I tell people that, they don't understand.

TALMADGE. How's that?

MEL. When first you fall in love you get this wide open pretty view. Seems so easy. Before you know it that big open view shrinks up, you can't see a thing. All you can feel are those underground currents, driving you every which way, tearing up your insides.

TALMADGE. *(Doesn't.)* I see.

MEL. I knew you would.

(Pause.)

TALMADGE. Here, let me give you one of my cards. (*Reaches in wallet.*) I'm Talmadge Slay. I'm with Byrobie, we're a young company but we're starting to make a mark with a new product called "Catch and Release" helps keep a fish alive through a stressful situation.

MEL. *(MEL studies the card, puts it away. Is at a loss as to what to give to Talmadge. Finally hands him his beanie shooter.)* Mel Whaley. (*THEY shake hands.*)

TALMADGE. Thank you.

(Pause. THEY both stare out at lake.)

MEL. Well. You take care now, Talmadge.

TALMADGE. You too, Mel.

MEL. (*Starts to go. Stops and turns around.*) Sorry 'bout your face.

TALMADGE. (*Doesn't understand.*) That's all right.

(MEL exits. TALMADGE looks at the beanie shooter, touches his band-aid. Ponders. LIGHTS fade.)

Scene 3

Early afternoon. RAMONA sits on another part of the shore, resting back against something. SHE has a snake bite on an upper inner thigh. TEALE is having great difficulty breathing; takes in steady wheezing gasps, can't talk.

EVELYN. Be still, Ramona. Don't move.

RAMONA. Sons of bitches.

EVELYN. Please don't move.

RAMONA. Can you believe this?

EVELYN. Teale ... I don't know whether you should go or I should. You stay here with Ramona. I'll try to flag down a car.

RAMONA. Where in blazes are my cigarettes.

EVELYN. I think the road is just up there. I'll be right back. Don't anybody leave. (*EVELYN exits.*)

RAMONA. Teale, you have a cigarette? (*TEALE inhales, wheezing.*) Sorry. Ain't we a pair. We've had some times, you and I, haven't we, Teale? Starting with that Indiana Invitational, Lake Patoka, first time you whooped me. Remember? Yeah, you remember.

EVELYN. (*Comes back.*) Teale, you go. I'll stay. Here, I'll write you a note. I don't have a pen. Does anybody have a pen? (*TEALE produces one from pocket.*) Piece of paper? Let me write on your hand, I'll write on your hand. What should I write? "Help. Snake bite." They'll think you have the snake bite. Here. (*Grabs other hand and writes.*) "Asthma." You okay? Can you do this? (*TEALE gives a thumbs up sign.*) Teale, you're the hero of the day I mean it.

(TEALE exits.)

RAMONA. How could I be so dumb. Is it swollen bad?

EVELYN. It's swollen.

RAMONA. It ought to be. That was one big snake, a western fucking diamondback. Jesus, but doesn't he have a flair?

EVELYN. How long ago were you bit?

RAMONA. I don't know. After the storm.

EVELYN. Christmas, that's over an hour ago.

RAMONA. I deserve this. I'm more mad at myself than I am at the snake. Hats off to you snake. You're a credit to your species, unlike me. I knew, I knew the second I stepped back into my boat he'd been there.

EVELYN. Your husband?

RAMONA. It was like my boat was trying to speak to me, warn me, send warning vibrations up my legs.

EVELYN. Why did you get out on shore?

RAMONA. Lightning. You see that lightning?

EVELYN. Correct me. You aren't afraid when someone shoots at you but you're afraid of lightning?

RAMONA. Lightning scares me to death. Someone shoots at you it's kind of flattering, there's some emotion behind it. There's no feeling behind lightning. You have any gum?

EVELYN. I have a Certs. I think I do.

RAMONA. Mouth is dry.

EVELYN. I think there's one left. (*Searches in pocket.*) Oh God, let there be one more left. There is. Here.

RAMONA. Thanks. Ow, ychh. This poison is hate, Evelyn, hot nasty hate coursing through me.

EVELYN. Should I cut it? I've got my Swiss army knife.

RAMONA. Are you good with a knife?

EVELYN. I can make florets out of melon balls.

RAMONA. Let's skip it. Shit, he knew I'd pull over and duck out the storm in that little cave up that arroyo. See, Evelyn, Willow Canyon has got some history to it. Five years ago, my second Classic win with my trusty Zara Spook, punctuated by one sweet intermission.

EVELYN. It's turning kind of green. Is that significant?

RAMONA. This year my Zara Spook landed me a snake.

EVELYN. Should I maybe suck on it, a little?

RAMONA. Couldn't hurt.

EVELYN. (*Bends down over the wound. SHE hesitates.*) It's all right if I get it on my lips? I just shouldn't swallow any, correct?

RAMONA. Correct.

(EVELYN bends over more; hesitates again.)

RAMONA. Let's forget it.

EVELYN. I'm happy to.

RAMONA. I appreciate that but let's not fool with it. Hey, I'm real sorry about this, blowing your chances for the tournament. I didn't even ask you how your fishing was going.

EVELYN. Don't be sorry. I didn't stand a chance anyway. Just caught one fish.

RAMONA. First one's most important.

EVELYN. She's a beauty. Must be carrying eggs. I never saw a fish so enormous, I think she might be a record fish. (*Looks off.*) I wonder how she's doing.

RAMONA. You catch a record fish you'll get rookie of the year.

EVELYN. Rookie, of the year? Me? I'm not the type.

RAMONA. Sure you are. Ow! I should have known if he wasn't in the cave in one mood then he'd be somewheres else in another mood. Got back in my boat, turned the key, wouldn't start. Went to check my engine, went to check my battery …

EVELYN. Rookie of the year.

RAMONA. … went to check my live well—I had four keepers, Evelyn, my water was holding up so nice—went to check my dry well. Why I don't know. Lifted up the lid and that snake was hanging from my thigh like it was born for it, like five generations in the family were bred special for the event.

EVELYN. Why did you pull over if you knew he'd be here? He tried to shoot you last night.

RAMONA. I figured that was just a little foreplay. That's what kills me. I'm ashamed to admit it. I was hoping he'd be here.

EVELYN. For what purpose?

RAMONA. Evelyn, have mercy. It's been rough. Ever since I moved to Atlanta the men I've dated have been … I don't know … malnourished. I mean, these people have had the animal bred out of them. They take you to bed like they're getting ready to collate you or something, like they're looking forward to later when they can set their digital clock Mr. Coffee machines. None of them *smell*. Ol' Mel, maybe he couldn't talk about nothing but snowbirds, beans, water, water, water—I used to tell him he had water on the brain, Jacques Costeau could do a underwater special in his mind—but the man had a smell that was pure genius.

EVELYN. Mm.

RAMONA. I tell you what … there was some powerful electricity between us. You get used to reading with a 150 watt bulb, a 20 watt bulb just isn't gonna hold your eye to the page.

EVELYN. Ramona … your complexion isn't too good.

RAMONA. What's wrong with it?

EVELYN. It's … well, it's … How'd he finagle the snake into your dry well?

RAMONA. That's what I'm trying to tell you. The man has good hands. If only he could have talked to me.

EVELYN. You can rest your head here.

RAMONA. (*Leans up against her.*) The man is incapable of sustained conversation. When he was a boy he'd spend days, weeks alone up in the mountains catching wild mustangs to sell. Wouldn't talk to anybody. Just his dog. Poor booger never learned how to talk, how to respond. Oh, he can tell you stories about his childhood, women always fall for them, but once the tape runs out that's it. He never updates. You never feel like you're in the present tense with him except when he's making love, and then ... first time I met him, I went off and was sick to my stomach for three days. It was that physical.

EVELYN. Goodness.

RAMONA. That's exactly right. Good-ness. And that's the shame of it, right there, that's the crying shame of it. You think that's enough, Evelyn? For a relationship? That's not enough, is it? I mean, I had cryosurgery on my cervix after a bad pap smear? He couldn't say one word to me about it. Not one related word. He waited out in the parking lot, I got in the truck, first thing he said after ten minutes driving home was he didn't know why everybody complained so much about the new Coca-cola formula he liked it.

EVELYN. He liked the new Coca-cola formula?

RAMONA. Yeah. Ow! Jesus ... *Christ*! I have suffered pain before but ...

EVELYN. Keep talking, Ramona. Tell me more about Mel.

RAMONA. He had a favorite nephew, Hardy, loved him like a son. He died. Drowned in less than two feet of water, drunk as a skunk. Mel was so busted up inside you could hear the pieces break apart. Think we could sit around and cry together, share memories, visit with Hardy's folks? That man sat for two days in his truck, parked up on the mesa, wouldn't eat, wouldn't talk, wouldn't go to the funeral or the cook-out.

EVELYN. Must have felt terrible.

RAMONA. I slept out in the back of the truck, waiting for him to come and talk to me. Saw two UFOs; you'll see them up there. Nearly froze to death. Listen to this, I had an affair with someone, told him about it, he just stood there and stared at me, stared like I wasn't even there, like I'd evaporated. I could see my reflection evaporate in his eyes. The opposite of tears.

EVELYN. You had an affair?

RAMONA. Aa, it was more an act of desperation. I was that lonesome.

EVELYN. Who with?

RAMONA. Some wimpy new age guy. I met him at the Seven Eleven. He offered to read my astrology chart. It was nice hearing someone discuss my life with me for a change, even if everything he said was wrong.

EVELYN. If I told Talmadge I'd had an affair, he'd get catatonic.

RAMONA. Never said a word. 'Course it wasn't too much later he shot both front tires of my old Bronco. Ow.

EVELYN. You know, could be Mel didn't plant that snake. Maybe it happened in on its own.

RAMONA. He did.

EVELYN. Maybe not. It's such a loathsome thing to do.

RAMONA. Oh well, now. He had his reasons. I'm no saint. Evelyn, I don't mean to get personal, but you know you really ought not to drink if you're pregnant.

EVELYN. I'm not pregnant.

RAMONA. You're not?

EVELYN. No.

RAMONA. No? Huh. I thought you were.

EVELYN. Why would you think that?

RAMONA. When we were driving down here. Had a real strong hit. Crossed my mind more'n once.

EVELYN. Well, I'm not.

RAMONA. Mm. Funny, I'm usually right on that one. Your fingers are twitching.

EVELYN. Sorry, I'm typing.

RAMONA. Uh-huh. (*Pause.*) You know, if and when you do get pregnant, you can keep right on fishing. No reason to stop.

EVELYN. How can you fish if you have a baby?

RAMONA. I did.

EVELYN. You did?

RAMONA. No nicer cradle than a rocking boat.

EVELYN. You took your baby fishing?

RAMONA. Yeah. Both of 'em. Evelyn, I feel inordinately bad. Think you could type me out of here? I'm starting to see two of you.

EVELYN. I'm going.

RAMONA. Evelyn?

EVELYN. Yeah?

RAMONA. Thanks.

EVELYN. Don't move.

RAMONA. Don't worry. I'm not going anywhere.

(EVELYN exits. RAMONA lies on her back, fading fast.)

RAMONA. I'm too sorely disappointed. Fish. Bait. Fish. Bait. Who is the fish. Who is the bait. Who is at what end of the line. Francis, come heal me. (*Starts crying softly. MEL enters out of her sight.)* I'm sorry, Mel. Sons of bitches. How can anyone so insensitive be so damn sensitive? (*Drifts off.*)

(MEL approaches Ramona. SHE senses his presence.)

RAMONA. Hey, Mel.
MEL. Western diamondback. *(Goes to the wound.)*
RAMONA. You should know.

(HE takes out knife, puts down his hat, cuts the wound, sucks it, wraps his bandana up above it.)

RAMONA. *(SHE winces with pain as HE treats the wound.)* Hillis tell you she stopped and visited me in Atlanta? Stayed a couple days, looked good. Said you'd moved out of town back to your old house up on the mesa. Not too lonely for you? How's your momma doing? I sent her a card Christmas. My old Bronco finally broke down, threw a bearing at the Peach Tree Plaza man you would really hate Atlanta. Guess I pissed you off, inviting you down for a rendezvous. I didn't mean any harm, Mel. That time last spring I called, said I'd meet you? I tried to get there. I tried. I just … couldn't. I wanted to.
MEL. Ramona. …
RAMONA. I did.

(THEY kiss. EVELYN enters.)

EVELYN. Ramona … *(Sees them. Stops.)*
RAMONA. Hey, Evelyn. Welcome wagon showed up.
MEL. Evelyn?
EVELYN. Yes.
MEL. That man who loves you? Talmadge Slay? He loves you.

EVELYN. Who is this person?

RAMONA. Evelyn, this is Mel.

EVELYN. Mel? *The* Mel? Snake Mel?

MEL. Snake Mel?

RAMONA. Nice move, putting a diamondback in my dry well. Nice.

MEL. You think I put it in there?

RAMONA. 'Course I do.

MEL. You think I could do such a thing?

RAMONA. You know, for a joke. Didn't you? Didn't you? (*MEL picks up his hat, gets up and walks away; hurt.*) Well, shoot, maybe I left the lid open. Forget it. My apologies, Mel. Must be the poison. Poison. (*Closes eyes.*) Must be delirious.

EVELYN. Mel. (*HE doesn't respond.*) Mel. Well. (*Pause.*) I guess we ought to hurry.

RAMONA. I'm sorry, baby. Don't take it to heart.

EVELYN. Time is of the essence. Isn't it? Mel, are you all right? I know she was looking forward to seeing you.

MEL. (*HE looks at Evelyn.*) She said that?

EVELYN. She said a lot of nice things about you. She said you had good hands. And you do. (*Embarrassed by her response to them.*) Have … good … hands.

(BOTH go to pick her up.)

MEL. Don't strain yourself, m'am. Not in your condition.

(HE embraces Ramona as HE carries her off. EVELYN is left staring out front.)

Scene 4

Mid afternoon. The sun is quite hot. MARGERY is in a phone booth in the desert in front of a motel whose sign, "Arroyo Seco Motel," might be seen in the distance behind the booth.

MARGERY. (*On the phone.*) Lydia? Lydia, I'm thinking of coming home. I don't know, I guess I used to be a lot braver. I've been in my motel room all day until now. I'm in this phone booth outside. Lydia, picture me out in the desert holding on to a phone booth, holding on. The view? It's terrifying. The sky, the desert, there's too much ... *space* it just goes on and on how do people adjust to this. Someone's waving over there. I woke up this morning in a cold sweat, a cold sweat. I *am* upset. There's this cow skull over my bed, not a Georgia O'Keefe cow skull, a real live dead cow skull. I was reading *Bonfire of the Vanities,* I could feel it staring at me so I put it in the closet. Immediately there was this disturbance in the room, like I'd tampered with some sacred spirit. I put it back up and the jawbone, Lydia, the jawbone broke off in my hands. There are forces down here bigger than you or I—what is that person doing—primitive, raw forces so natural they're unnatural. No. No galleries, no jewelry, just a vast amount of vastness, my stomach, how did the pioneers ever make it to California. I feel like such a failure. I haven't been into town I don't have a car, some psychopath with a beanie shooter let me off here last night. What? I was going to go to Santa Fe my travel agent talked me into coming down here; she had some healing experience at these hot springs the Indians used to go to to bathe their wounds, I don't know. This is where the first atomic bomb ever exploded, Lydia, that's the kind of energy I'm talking about. Could you wait a sec, hon. (*Steps out of booth, looking.*) Someone is behaving very bizarrely, they're probably on mushrooms. Oh my God, he's coming over here.

(TEALE enters; if possible from a distance. SHE is crawling, wearing her hair up under her cap, breathing rapidly, gasping loudly as she inhales. As SHE crawls toward Margery, SHE might stop, rest her head on her arm on the floor, wave.)

MARGERY. I don't know, some little man. I don't know, he's just ... what a nightmare. Lydia, could you get a pen. Quick, quick get a pen. You have one? Pencil's fine write down this number. Shit! There's no number here, I'm somewhere with no number, God. Please deposit fifty cents? I just did, I just did deposit fifty cents, operator. Operator? I don't have any more chan ... operator? (*Searching through her bag.*) Lydia, what should I do? Uh, here's a quarter ... (*Deposits two quarters.*) Thank God. Don't hang up. (*SHE steps out of booth and addresses TEALE who has just arrived and is holding on to the booth, still on the ground, still gasping.*) Excuse me, can I help you? Por favor? (*Into phone.*) I think she wants to use the phone. It's a woman. (*To Teale.*) I'll just be a few more minutes.

(SHE closes the door. TEALE stands, opens the door, takes the receiver and hangs up, pinning Margery in the process.)

MARGERY. That's fine, I was finished anyway.

(MARGERY starts to bolt and TEALE grabs her with one hand and dials 911 with the other.)

MARGERY. Are you all right? (*TEALE hands the phone to Margery and gets down on the ground again; crawls forward out of the booth.*) Hello? This is Margery Caldwell, to whom am I speaking please? Oh. Oh, could you send an ambulance right away, someone here is in great difficulty. I'm not sure, she's having trouble breathing. What? Uh, the Arroyo Seco Motel; it's near ... nothing. Fine. Thank you very much. (*Hangs up.*) They're on their way. (*TEALE is still gasping loudly.*) Try to relax. Take a deep breath.

(SHE does so herself. MARGERY helps her up so that TEALE is standing, hugging her with both arms around her. THEY both breathe together.)

MARGERY. I'll come in the ambulance with you. (*TEALE tries to thank her.*) Oh, don't thank me. I needed a ride into town anyway. (*LIGHTS fade.*)

Scene 5

The stage of a high school auditorium. EVELYN is standing at the microphone dressed in a long gown. A Bass'n Gal banner might hang behind her.

EVELYN. (*Clasping trophy.*) Am I thrilled. I feel like I'm all the way up on the high dive. Larry Bottroff has informed me that she definitely is a state record, possibly the second largest bass ever recorded but we need to verify it with the department of fish and game. 27.9 inches in length, 25 inches in girth, 21 pounds 9.44 ounces. Egg laden sow black bass, between 13 and 15 years old. Old enough to be in high school. Be a cheerleader. Talmadge, are you here? Rookie of the year. I am truly honored.

She died ... about an hour ago. We kept her alive for a good length of time with that new product Catch and Release, helps keep a fish alive through a stressful situation. It's the same effect as drinking Gatorade. I recommend it. She is a real beauty. Most of you have seen her but if you haven't and you want to, she's in the big walk-in cooler at the back of the cafeteria, up on the shelf over the juices. Just ask Olive, she'll show you where, or her husband Bennie. You can find him at maintenance. Or I'll show you. You can find me ... in the stars. I always heard the Classic was the ultimate and now I know it's true.

I want to thank Ramona and Teale for their support. I'm sorry they can't be here now. They're both still in the hospital. Room 204 you can visit them. Right above the juices, just kidding. And Margery, I want to thank Margery for all her help, some of you have met her, she pitched in with the decorations. And I want to thank Talmadge for giving me that fishing pole for Mother's Day three years ago, just a week after we met. He gave me a real nice rod, he knew I wanted one, and this fish bowl with green Jello in it, green Jello with little Pepperidge Farm cracker fish floating in it, suspended in the Jello. It was just darling. And he gave me a box of scented tissues which was real sweet of him 'cause I was still wrought up over Mister B. I have this little dachshund, Mister B. I call him Mister B. for Mister Big cause he's so small. What happened was this pack of wild dogs got him and drug him up the mountain up one end and back down the other. He managed to get home but he was real depressed; all bloody and some of his ribs were broken. They'd punctured his lungs. I knew if I took him to the vet that would be the end of him. They put them in those cages, you know, and given his mental state I knew he wouldn't make it so I just held him all night. When their lungs are punctured the air comes right up under the skin. I could feel it. So, I just started to squish him. I squished him and squished him, you know like when you pop those mailer sheets? Well, he made it. The next day I took him to the vet and he said I'd done the right thing, squishing that air back down inside him. Seemed like all he wanted was to be in my arms. Egg laden sow bass. Kind of sad ... Anyhow. This is my first trophy ever. I did get a trivet once for a door prize but it doesn't mean diddlysquat to me. So. I don't want this moment to end. I don't want to get down.

TALMADGE. (*Yelling from back of auditorium; just arrived.*) Evelyn!

EVELYN. Talmadge, where are you?

TALMADGE. I'm here, honey. I made it!

EVELYN. Are you okay?

TALMADGE. Yeah.

EVELYN. Where have you been? I've been worried sick, I looked everywhere for you. Where were you?

TALMADGE. I was asleep.

EVELYN. Asleep?

TALMADGE. I haven't slept in two nights, Evie.

EVELYN. Talmadge, how could you be asleep? I'm rookie of the year.

TALMADGE. Rookie of the year! Yes, Evie! All right!

EVELYN. You almost missed it.

TALMADGE. I didn't miss it, sweetheart. I'm here.

EVELYN. You had me so worried. You've never not been there. Don't come up here. (*HE keeps approaching the stage.*) Talmadge. Talmadge, don't come up here this is my stage! And it was my trip, my big trip to New Mexico, you were wrong to barrel in and drive me and Teale out here.

TALMADGE. What?

EVELYN. You knew how much that trip meant to me, you knew. You watched all I did to get ready for it. I had Grady show me how to change a flat, I bought all those things, my atlas, my Mobile guide to emergency repairs, I practiced my driving. You don't even know I was going to drive west on 64, take the Blue Ridge Parkway over to 65 and then shoot down to 40 not just go straight plunk down 77 as you did without asking me my opinion.

TALMADGE. I'm sorry, Evie.

EVELYN. I'm driving my car home, Talmadge. I'm driving the whole way. In whatever gear I like.

TALMADGE. Okay, okay. I'm really sorry. I am. I was scared to death to let you go.

EVELYN. Talmadge, you are going to have to get over being scared to death. I'm not a china doll, I can weather a crisis without you.

TALMADGE. That's what I'm afraid of.

EVELYN. That's what you're afraid of? Talmadge, just because there are times I don't need you doesn't mean I don't need you.

TALMADGE. Really?

EVELYN. Of course. (*Notices the audience.*) Oh my Lord. Excuse me so much, everyone. I didn't mean to hog the stage. Thank you all very much, now I'll get down.

TALMADGE. Evie, you look so beautiful.

EVELYN. Wait till you see my fish. (*SHE smiles at him.*) I have something nice to tell you later. (*To audience.*) So long everyone. See you on the tour. (*Holding up trophy.*) Rookie of the year!

Scene 6

Later that night, after the banquet, in Evelyn's car. EVELYN, wearing a jacket over her gown, is driving with ostensible concentration. MARGERY sits next to her, wearing Teale's cap. TEALE is in the back seat holding a cooler with the fish in it on her lap, next to TALMADGE who holds the trophy and gazes out the window.

MARGERY. You're so nice to give me a ride, I really appreciate it.

EVELYN. No trouble.

MARGERY. It's out here somewhere, I know it is. I think it's going to be on the right.

TALMADGE. What does your husband do, Margery?

MARGERY. My husband? He has affairs with young women.

TALMADGE. I'm sorry, I didn't hear you.

MARGERY. He has affairs with very young women. The younger the better.

TALMADGE. Ah. I did hear you correctly.

MARGERY. There it is.

(Pause.)

TALMADGE. There's no one behind you, sweetheart. Sweetheart, there's no one behind you.

EVELYN. These mirrors are all out of whack. Where's the driveway?

TALMADGE. There is no driveway.

EVELYN. There's no driveway?

TALMADGE. Just pull in, sweetheart. Evie, you're going to pass it.

EVELYN. I don't want to go over the curb.

TALMADGE. There is no curb.

EVELYN. No curb?

MARGERY. I think you can just pull over, Evelyn.

EVELYN. I'll stop here. (*SHE brakes. ALL lurch forward.*)

MARGERY. Perfect. (*MARGERY gets out of the car. TEALE does, too, holding cooler so she can get in front seat.*) Thanks so much, I had a great time. Really, I had a ball. Talmadge, would you mind taking a picture of me with everyone?

TALMADGE. Sure thing. (*HE gets out.*)

MARGERY. This will go right over my desk. With the fish, Teale. With the fish. No, no, in the cooler's fine. Evelyn, you hold the trophy. (*Showing him the camera.*) Just push down right here. (*THEY pose.*) Great. One more? Thanks. (*THEY get back in car.*) Teale, I'm serious about you coming to New York. I'm sending you an open round trip ticket and you're coming and that's that. Just let me know when.

EVELYN. We'll wait till you get inside.

MARGERY. That's okay. I think I'll go for a walk. It's such a beautiful night.

TALMADGE. You might not ought to walk alone out here.

MARGERY. Is this spectacular? Look at all this ... space. It goes on and on and on. This. This is what I came out here for.

EVELYN. Well, we need to get rolling.

MARGERY. Drive carefully, Evelyn. So long, everyone. God bless.

ALL. Bye, Margery. Bye. Adios. Take care. See you.

(SHE exits. THEY continue driving.)

TEALE. (*Studying Rand McNally map with flashlight.*) Okay, Evelyn, it's straight for a long time; next turn's a couple hundred miles. (*Looking in cooler.*) I think Fred Claire up in Buxton does a nice job of taxidermy. Avery's older brother? You sure you want me to have her?

EVELYN. I want you to have her.

TEALE. (*Studying fish.*) Imagine trying to breath through little slits in your sides. Tell you what, that's just about how I felt out there. Gasping like a fish out of water, felt like I was breathing through my buttonholes. But you know what, you come out the other side of something like that, you feel a whole lot lighter. Rookie of the year.

EVELYN. Teale, could you put this cassette in?

TEALE. Sure.

(MUSIC up of Talmadge's song; HE whistles the first verse under Teale's words.)

TEALE. I was thinking of Ramona's wallpaper on the universe, everyone's own familiar pattern? And I was thinking of how you'd strip it. With vinegar and hot water, splashing it on up, peeling it off. And on the other side of the paper there'd be all this ... space ... and stars ... and you could just keep going. And going.

(Cassette player:)

Sweetheart, I sing this song to you
While you're out on the road
To tell you of a love that's true
And of a love that's bold

My darlin', know I miss you
I'm thinking of you now
And if I could, I'd kiss you
Upon your gentle brow

EVELYN. *(Turning it down.)* Thanks for the song, Talmadge. It's real pretty.

TEALE. He's asleep.

EVELYN. Teale. I'm pregnant.

TEALE. Ramona says it's a girl. Highly evolved on the spiritual plane. I hope she likes to fish.

EVELYN. Could you reach back there and cover him up with that blanket?

(EVELYN turns up the cassette again as TEALE covers up Talmadge with a blanket.)

My song will keep you company
As through the night you ride
You're never far away from me
Imagine me nearby

Oh, Evelyn I love you
Your lips, your hair, your eyes
If I were in a tournament
You'd be my first prize.

(LIGHTS are fading slowly to BLACK.
Switch to up-beat MUSIC for curtain call. Then play Talmadge's song from the top as audience exits.)

COSTUME PLOT

TALMADGE
(Look #1)
Off-white t-shirt
Tan stripe pajama bottoms
Green company jacket with Byrobie logo
Distressed sneakers
No socks
(Look #2)
Off-white t-shirt
Gold sweatshirt with Santa Fe logo
White cotton shorts
Bass'n Gal cap
Distressed sneakers

MEL
Jeans
Red and grey plaid poly-cotton western shirt with snaps
Cowboy boots
Tooled cowboy belt with large rodeo buckle and "Mel" across back
Hat, if needed

RAMONA
(Car and campsite scenes)
Bra
Panties
Red and black lace camisole
Tapered light blue jeans
Pale green rayon shit with floral detail

Teal windbreaker with "Ramona" on chest and patches
Tan western boots
Earrings
Thin belt
(Snakebite scene)
Bra
White long-sleeved camp shirt with sleeves rolled up
Khaki vest with winners patches
Second pair of jeans with ripped side seam on the right leg
Fishing cap
Rebok sneakers
Earrings
Blue cotton bandanna

TEALE
(Car, house, and return scenes)
Bra
Blue jeans with button fly
Blue and yellow striped cotton shirt
Pale yellow cotton windbreaker
Sneakers
Beige handbag
(Campfire)
Bra
Loose shirt
Loose jeans
Add blue sweat pants
Black hooded hummingbird sweatshirt
Sneakers

(Fishing and phone scenes)
Bra
Jeans
Yellow hummingbird t-shirt
Blue short-sleeved patchpocket shirt
Sneakers

EVELYN
(Bedroom, car, campsite scenes)
Bra
Panties
Big shirt nightgown with stripes
Khaki pull-on sport pants
Blue oxford shirt
Teal cotton windbreaker
Sneakers
Purse
(Pants, shirt, sneakers, jacket are put on during scene)
(Fishing scene)
Bra
Panties
White camp shirt with sponsor patches
Khaki cotton shorts
Cap
Sneakers
(Award ceremony scene)
Bra
Panties
Shorts (underdressed)
Loose shirt
Blue floral print acetate long gown with belt

Hair worn up
Blue pumps
Earrings
Necklace
(Return in car scene)
Bra
Panties
Shorts (underdressed)
Fast change: Loose dress, pink satin Bass'n Gal jacket
Sneakers

MARGERY
(Car scene)
Bra
Lime green silk knit blouse with gold chain detail
Tan pleated cotton pants
Tan woven flats
Ornate hip belt
Santa Fe earrings
(Phone booth scene)
Bra
Blue t-shirt with tropical floral motif
Tan pleated cotton pants
Tan woven flats
One earring

PROPERTY PLOT

ACT I

breakfast tray
breakfast food
glass of orange juice
two boxes of pop tarts
cup of coffee
toaster
balloon
3 wrapped presents
wrapped cassette
3 alarm clocks
hairbrush
Evie's duffel bag
cassette player
road atlas
purse with driving gloves
2 asthma medicines
banjo
Coke
peanuts
beanie shooter (slingshot)
beer
2 lanterns
3 sleeping bags
Teale's harmonica
Ramona's fishing rods
Ramona's tackle box
fish perfume
lures

topographic map
alarm clock
lure grippers
Ramona's duffel bag
Teale's duffel bag
bottle Jack Daniels
rice crispie bars
roll of toilet paper
swiss army knife
fish hooks
cigarettes
bandaid
gun
fishing line

ACT II

boat seat for Teale
cooler with sandwich, soda
Evelyn's tackle box
note with candy valentine heart
ph meter
binoculars
sunscreen
fishing net
two fishing rods
rifle
wallet
business card
beanie shooter (slingshot)
pen
bandana

swiss army knife
Certs
Mel's knife
phone booth
filofax
pocket change
trophy
mid stand
penlight
road atlas
camera
cooler